Pan-Africanism, Gender Emancipation and the Meaning of Socialist Development

Revisiting the role of women in Kwame Nkrumah's Ghana

By Abayomi Azikiwe
Editor, Pan-African News Wire

During July 1960 an historic gathering of African women from throughout the continent and Diaspora took place in Accra, Ghana. This West African state had been liberated from British colonialism just three years before under the leadership of the Convention People's Party (CPP) headed by Dr. Kwame Nkrumah.

This Conference of the Women of Africa and African Descent (CWAAD) passed resolutions calling for many of the same objectives as previous Pan-African gatherings in Ghana and other parts of Africa. The CPP was in a better position than any other party on the continent to set the stage and provide a sterling example as it related to gender equality.

Nkrumah said to African women in his opening address to the CWAAD that: "Your role in this direction is of great importance. Not only can you carry back this message to the men of your respective countries, but, if you are convinced that unity is the right answer, you can also bring your feminine influence to bear in persuading your brothers, husbands and friends of the importance of Africa unity as the only salvation for Africa. For my part, I stand resolutely and inexorably by this conviction and will work with unrelenting determination for its attainment.
There is a great responsibility resting on the shoulders of all women of Africa and African descent. They must realize that the men alone cannot complete the gigantic task we have set ourselves. The time has come when the women of Africa and of African descent must rise up in their millions to join the Africa crusade for freedom."

Women were in the forefront of the movement for national liberation in Ghana, then known as the Gold Coast prior to 1957. The early efforts of Nkrumah sought the full participation of women in the initial phases of organizing with the United Gold Coast Convention (UGCC) and the Committee on Youth Organization (CYO).

Although it was the UGCC which invited Nkrumah back to the Gold Coast his organizing efforts would place him at loggerheads with its middle-class and royalist leadership. The formation of the CYO mobilized the students and youth of the country along the lines of Pan-Africanism and immediate national liberation. By June 1949, the supporters of Nkrumah urged that he form a political organization to demand independence now. The CPP was launched on June 12, 1949 with 60,000 people in attendance and consequently from its initiation the party was a mass force playing a vanguard role in the struggle for national liberation from British imperialism.

Historical events since Nkrumah had left the Gold Coast for the U.S. in 1935 served to catapult him into national and international prominence. Nkrumah had returned to the Gold Coast from a two year stay in England where he studied at the London School of Economics and organized the historic Fifth Pan-African Congress in Manchester held in October 1945. The gathering was characterized by the emergence of a mass Pan-Africanist movement led by revolutionary intellectuals, students, workers and farmers.

Prior to his stay in Britain, Nkrumah had studied for ten years in the United States from 1935-1945. He obtained undergraduate and graduate degrees from the Historical Black University of Lincoln in Pennsylvania and the University of Pennsylvania. As a student Nkrumah led the African Students Association of the U.S. and Canada, wrote for student and academic newsletters and journals, belonging to numerous left-wing and anti-imperialist groups including the Council on African Affairs (CAA), the Universal Negro

Improvement Association (African Communities League), among others. His tenure also involved the study of theology and the licensing as a Presbyterian minister where he traveled extensively speaking in African American churches.

Some of the most advanced organizers and party propagandist within the CPP were women from its inception extending to the overthrow of the Nkrumah government on February 24, 1966 at the aegis of the U.S. Central Intelligence Agency (CIA) utilizing disgruntled elements within the Ghanaian military and police. Over the course of the period between 1948 and 1966, CPP women held positions as journalists, intelligence operatives, fundraisers and political officials.

The Conference of the Women of Africa and African Descent was convened on the initiative of the Ghana Women's movement represented by the consolidation of the two main organizations concerned with gender issues in 1960. The CPP (Ghana) Women's League and the National Federation of Ghana Women merged to form the National Council of Ghana Women at the urging of the Nkrumah and the party leadership.

The Women's League was a CPP-led organization where the Federation, led by Secretary General Dr. Evelyn Amarteifio, was perceived as being more politically independent. The League was directed by CPP Propaganda Secretary Hannah Cudjoe who served as the principal organizer of the CWAAD in July 1960. Cudjoe had been recruited by Nkrumah doing the early days of the UGCC work and when the British arrested the top leaders of the group in the aftermath of a national strike and rebellion in February 1948, led protests demanding their release.

On an institutional level the leadership of the CPP as early as May 1951 in the wake of the release of Kwame Nkrumah from a one-year prison term for his anti-colonialist activities and the party's triumph in the local elections earlier that February, the mass independence party had appointed four women: Letitia Quaye, Miss Sophia Doku, Hannah Cudjoe and Ama Nkrumah, as propaganda secretaries charged with the duty of organizing women and others. During the period surrounding the convening of the All-African Women's Conference, the Ghanaian parliament at the aegis of the CPP passed the Representation of the People (Women Members) Bill in 1960. The legislation was passed on June 16, 1960.

This act facilitated the unopposed election of ten women as Members of Parliament (MPs). These women were Susana Al-Hassan, Ayanori Bukari and Victoria Nyarko, all representing the Northern Region, Sophia Doku and Mary Koranteng, Eastern Region, and Regina Asamany, Volta Region. The others were Grace Ayensu and Christiana Wilmot, Western Region, Comfort Asamoah, Ashanti Region, and Lucy Anim, Brong Ahafo. Later in 1965, Dr. Nkrumah appointed Madam Susan Al-Hassan as the Minister of Social Welfare and Community Development, while other women were appointed as district commissioners.

Consequently, the Conference gathering attracted hundreds of women who were playing an integral part in the national liberation process in Ghana, across Africa and the world. Delegations attended the Conference from various geo-political regions of the continent. From outside of Africa there was representation from the United States where the likes of Shirley Graham Du Bois attended and delivered an important policy address.

Shirley Graham DuBois, the second wife of W.E.B. DuBois and an accomplished writer, organizer and committed socialist in her own right, was in Ghana at the time of the founding of the First Republic along with the inauguration of the NCGW and the Conference of Women of Africa and African Descent. She stated in an address before the Women's Association of the Socialist Students Organizations in Ghana that "the advancement of Ghanaian women in recent years has been amazing and now with ten women Parliamentarians in Republican Ghana, this country had achieved what took Europe centuries to accomplish." (Evening News, July 14, 1960)

In supporting the-then movement toward socialism in Ghana, DuBois recounted her travels to the People's Republic of China and the achievements of women since the revolution of 1949. She noted in her address "the women of Socialist China were advanced in all spheres of useful activity and enjoyed equal rights with men politically, economically, culturally, socially and domestically."

Kwame Nkrumah in delivering the opening address to the Conference of the Women of Africa and African Descent on July 18, 1960 said: "I am indeed happy to be here this morning to open such a conference. Who would have thought that in this year of 1960, it would be possible to even hold a conference of all Ghanaian women, much less of women of all Africa and African descent! But today, that is a reality and an achievement which constitutes another landmark of progress in Africa's irresistible march to emancipation and victory."

The president and leader of the CPP went on to note that: "All of you are aware of the present trend in Africa. The whole continent is ablaze with the fire of nationalism. This great giant Africa, which was anaesthetized for so long, is now awake and has shaken itself out of the slumber that for so many years enabled exploiters and marauders to plunder its wealth. The new African has arrived on the scene. Colonialism and imperialism are on the run, fleeing from the blows of African irredentism. What is woman's part in the great struggle for African liberation? You have to provide an answer to that question. But I can say something of the role adopted by Ghanaian womanhood in the past. The women of Ghana have played a most glorious part in our struggle for independence. They were solidly behind the Ghana revolution. Guided by the Convention People's Party, thousands of our women flocked to the nationalist banners and, side by side with the men, fought heroically until freedom was achieved for Ghana."

This trend towards national liberation and Pan-Africanism was not confined to Ghana alone. In South African under the vicious system of apartheid-colonialism women had led the anti-pass campaigns of the early 1950s. In 1954, the Federation of South African Women (FEDSAW) was formed bringing together progressive forces within the African, Colored, Indian and white communities in alliance with the African National Congress. Women were indicted under the treason trials that were held against the revolutionary democratic movement between the years of 1956-1960.

On August 9, 1956, 20,000 South African women marched against racism and national oppression in Pretoria setting the stage for a broadening of the mass struggle against the exploitation and repression of the apartheid system. Within the ANC as an organization there was a process of historical transformation that mirrored the development of the nationalist movement from its beginnings in the early decades of the 20th century until the post-World War II period.

Although in the Gold Coast (Ghana) during the incipient phase of the development of the CPP under Nkrumah, women were in the leadership of the party as organizers, journalists, propagandists and fundraisers, the situation was quite different in relationship to the ANC, which was formed as the South African Native National Council on January 8, 1912 in Bloemfontein in the Orange Free State.

According to the South African History website, "When the African National Congress (ANC) was formed in 1912, it did not accept women as members. In 1918, the government threatened to reintroduce pass laws for women that had been relaxed after the success of earlier resistance to passes. In the light of these events, the Bantu Women's League (BWL) was formed in 1918, as a branch of the ANC. It became involved in passive resistance and fought against passes for Black women. During this time the Bantu

Women's League was under the leadership of Charlotte Maxeke. The ANC only accepted women as members at the Congress's 1943 conference and in 1948 the ANC Women's League was formed. The first official president of the League was Ida Mntwana who was appointed after a brief stint by Madie Hall-Xuma.

This same site goes on to note: "The women became active in the Defiance Campaign of 1952 where they played a leading role. In the Eastern Cape 1067 of the 2529 defiers were women, with Florence Matomela at the forefront. The Women's League was then asked by the Congress Alliance to assist in organizing the 1955 Congress of the People, where the Freedom Charter was to be adopted. This gave the women an opportunity to lobby for the incorporation of their demands into the charter. In 1955, the issue of passes came forth again as the government announced that it would start issuing reference books from January 1956. A demonstration was held on the 27th of October 1955 and was attended by 2 000 women. On the 9th of August 1956, the women of the league confronted Prime Minister J.G. Strydom, under the auspices of the Federation of South African Women with a petition against pass laws." (http://www.sahistory.org.za/topic/anc-womens-league-ancwl)

In Egypt during the 1919 uprising against British imperialism, women came into the streets in the thousands. Nabila Ramdani has researched the intersection between Egyptian nationalism and feminism tracing back the role of women in literary, cultural and political circles into the late 19th century.

Ramdani emphasized in a research paper that: "During the 1919 Revolution, Huda Sha'arawi led veiled women demonstrators in the struggle against the British. Female solidarity with the Egyptian nationalists was exemplified by Sha'arawi's close collaboration with Sa'ad Zaghlul (1859-1927), leader of the Wafd ('delegation') – the Egyptian nationalist movement which was formed in 1918 at the end of the First World War. It was at the forefront of the push for independence from Britain, with both men and women lending their support to the 'party of the nation'. What women also made clear, however, was that they were equally campaigning for equality of the sexes – so engaging in a 'dual struggle'. Egyptian women first took part in nationalist demonstrations in March 1919, but they were to become crucial to the partial removal of the British from Egypt in 1922." (Journal of Women's Studies, March 2013, Vol. 14, Article 5)

Women's participation in other nationalists and Pan-Africanist struggles were also notable in Nigeria with the rebellion of women in the southeast region of the country in 1929. The British had consolidated control of what became known as Nigeria in 1914 through a system of indirect rule which facilitated the super-exploitation of the African people.

According to blackpast.org, "The "riots" or the war, led by women in the provinces of Calabar and Owerri in southeastern Nigeria in November and December of 1929, became known as the 'Aba Women's Riots of 1929' in British colonial history, or as the 'Women's War' in Igbo history. Thousands of Igbo women organized a massive revolt against the policies imposed by British colonial administrators in southeastern Nigeria, touching off the most serious challenge to British rule in the history of the colony. The 'Women's War' took months for the government to suppress and became a historic example of feminist and anti-colonial protest. The roots of the riots evolved from January 1, 1914, when the first Nigerian colonial governor, Lord Lugard, instituted the system of indirect rule in Southern Nigeria. Under the plan British administrators would rule locally through 'warrant chiefs,' essentially Igbo individuals appointed by the governor. Traditionally Igbo chiefs had been elected."

After the independence of several states within North Africa, with the exception of Algeria, which waged an armed struggle against French imperialism from 1954-1961, where women played a pivotal role as well, along with the breaking away of Sudan in 1956 and the

Gold Coast the following year, Nkrumah and other African leaders convened the First Conference of Independent African States in Accra from April 15-22, 1958. The gathering was chaired by Nkrumah and attended mainly by foreign ministers of the-then existing independent states of the United Arab Republic (Egypt), Libya, Tunisia, Morocco, Sudan, Liberia and Ethiopia.

This conference paved the way for the All-African People's Conference of December 1958 in Accra which attracted participation from 62 independence organizations and sovereign states. The AAPC was held under the banner of "Hands off Africa!" Several political figures in attendance would later become prominent in the struggle for national liberation, Pan-Africanism and Socialism, such as Patrice Lumumba of the Belgian Congo and Dr. Frantz Fanon of Martinique in the Caribbean.

Both Lumumba and Fanon would be dead by 1961. Lumumba was overthrown in the machinations of imperialist politics of 1960. By January 1961, he had been kidnapped, tortured and murdered by agents of Belgium, the U.S., Britain and other western states. Fanon died in the U.S. from leukemia after serving as an ambassador and editor for the National Liberation Front (FLN) of Algeria.

The decolonization process would prove to be violent one. Nkrumah and other revolutionaries in Ghana served prison time during the late 1940s. In Algeria, the French engaged in a series of massacres from the period of World War II through the early 1960s. South Africans were gunned down at Sharpeville in March 1960. In Congo, Lumumba and his comrades, Maurice Mpolo and Joseph Okito, would be assassinated amid a counterinsurgency war that destroyed the liberated territories in the vast country that sought to make real the vision of Lumumba and other revolutionary nationalists and Pan-Africanists.

However, 1960 was later designated as the "Year of Africa" where eighteen former colonies gained some form of national independence. Ghana extended its sovereignty by moving from an independent state within the Commonwealth to a Republic on July 1, 1960. Therefore the convening of the Conference of the Women of Africa and African Descent was in line with the continental and global struggle for African emancipation.

Women's Emancipation and the Convention People's Party (CPP)

Within this politico-historical context the CPP in Ghana would have been the ideal sponsors for such a conference. Women were already taking on leading positions within national liberation and Pan-Africanist movements throughout the continent and the Diaspora as Ghana was considered the citadel of the independence movements sweeping Africa and the Diaspora.

The CPP women were maintaining their role as propagandists and recruiters for the party in 1960. In a report published by the Evening News, a state-sponsored party newspaper started by Nkrumah in 1948 even prior to the formation of the CPP, in a section entitled "Party News and Notes" it says: "Madam Ardua Ankrah of Korie Wokon alias "Mrs. Nkrumah", continues her membership drive in Accra with increasing vigor. More U.P. (United Party opposition group) adherents at Ayalolo and Amamomo have approached her for enrollment into the dynamic CPP. Yesterday a delegation of 27 members from James Town called at her home and asked for admission into the CPP. In a short address Madam Ardua said to them, 'This is not a time for play. It is a time for hard work in the interest of Ghana. Dr. Kwame Nkrumah who released us from foreign bondage has again committed himself to the task of freeing us economically. Let us all unite as one man and follow Dr. Nkrumah even unto death.'" (Jan. 14, 1960, p. 5)

Earlier that same month on January 6, a photograph in the Evening News on page 10 under the headline "Evenews Picture Page" it depicts "Madam Lydia Addo, an organizer of the Convention People's Party, seen addressing a rally at the Bukom Square yesterday." This photograph appears alongside four others illustrating the first overhead bridge in Accra which was nearing completion on Boundary road near the Makola Market; the Omanhen of Sefwi, Wiawso Nana Kwadwo Aduhene, who was celebrating his annual yam festival; Minister of Finance K.A. Gbedemah, a co-founder of the CPP, who later fled into exile after the dockworkers strike of September 1961; and Bediako Poku, the Ghana ambassador to Israel who had served for two years as the General Secretary of the CPP.

A major source for the political recruitment of party cadres and the financing of its organizational work was the strategic role of the market women of Accra. C.L.R. James, the Trinidadian-born Marxist-Leninist historian and political analyst, said of the situation in Ghana during the anti-colonial and post-colonial phase that "one market woman was worth any dozen Achimota graduates," many of which were hostile to the national liberation movement. (Nkrumah and the Ghana Revolution, 1976)

In the January 2, 1960 edition of the Evening News a brief article entitled "Nkrumah Chats With Guests" it reports "Varieties of Ghanaian dishes were served at a luncheon party organized by the Life Chairman of the Convention People's Party, Dr. Kwame Nkrumah, in honor of members of the Ghana Market Women Traders Association and members of the women section of the CPP at the Flagstaff House in Accra. As the party progressed, Dr. Nkrumah who is also Life Patron of the Market Women Traders Association spent several minutes chatting with his guests. Proposing a toast on behalf of the women at the party, Madam Rebecca Dedei Aryeetey, Special Women Organizer to the Life Chairman of the CPP and the Association, assured Premier Nkrumah and his Government, the support of the 50,000 market women of this country." (Peter Plange, p. 6)

Leading up to the convening of the Women's conference in July 1960 tense negotiations between the Federation and the League resulted in the founding of the National Council of Ghana Women (NCGW). The task related to the merger of the two women's organization is recounted in a political biography by Tawia Adamafio, the former Vice-Chair of the CPP who would later in August 1962 fall from grace within the party after being accused by Nkrumah of being involved in an assassination attempt against the Osagyefo in the northern town of Kulungugu near the border with Upper Volta.

Adamafio stated in his book published in 1982 entitled "By Nkrumah's Side: The Labor and the Wounds", that he was forced into leading negotiations for the merger between the Federation and the League. He expresses fear over the role of women within the party saying they could become such a force as to neutralize the men leaders.

Nkrumah suggests to Adamafio that: "Our women must take over completely as private
secretaries, stenographers and copy typists. They should branch into engineering services, pharmacy, bus and taxi driving, law and medicine and all the other fields. They should go shoulder to shoulder with our men. At the time, and as Adamafio explains, there were two large women's groups in the country, one led by Dr. Evelyn Amarteifio and the other, the Ghana
Women's League, led by Hannah Kudjoe. Nkrumah wanted all women's groups in one organization: 'We must organize the women . . . as a distinct identity and keep them under our wings.'" (Jean Allman, "The Disappearing of Hannah Cudjoe: Nationalism, Feminism and the Tyrannies of History")

In the Adamafio book he further describes the challenge put before him by Nkrumah leading up the Conference of the Women of Africa and African Descent saying: "The Party women's solidarity was so all-inclusive when organized, that nothing could escape its steam-roller pressure. The Party women could not be bullied into submission by any party leader including Nkrumah himself on any matter…. If necessary the women did not hesitate to boo me or any other leader for that matter, and cause severe embarrassment and confusion to achieve their objective. . . . No, I cannot adequately convey to you an expression of the actual difficulty involved in organizing women, but if you could imagine their gossip, bitter quarrels and bickering and the acrimony of the lashing tongues, you would be getting nearer the truth than I could describe. I did not cherish this new task at all."

From Adamafio's account of the period the women within the two organizations exercised significant degrees of independence of thought and action. He says of the discussions among male members of the party and trade union movement that: "We foresaw a situation where this NCGW [National Council of Ghana Women] would grow so monolithic and powerful that the party could lose control of it. When you had its leadership bristling with dynamic women intellectuals and revolutionaries and the organization had become conscious of its strength, it could break off in rebellion, form a party by itself and sweep everything before it at the polls. The ratio of women voters to men then was about three or more to one and the position could well arise, where Ghana would be ruled by a woman President and an all-woman cabinet and the principal secretaries and Regional Commissioners were all women and men would be relegated to the back room! It would be disastrous for Ghana, for, I could see men being ridden like horses! A male tyrant could be twisted round a woman's little finger. An Amazonian tyrant could only probably be subdued by a battery of artillery!"

These stories reflect the role of Hanah Cudjoe, Ardua Ankrah, Lydia Addo and other women as public speakers, community organizers and recruiters. An understanding of these factors is essential to grasping even a rudimentary view of the growth and influence of the CPP. Ghana as a result of the national development policies of Nkrumah became the most advanced country in Africa during the 1950s and 1960s in part by emphasizing primary, secondary and higher educational attainment. Over a period of a six year transition from 1951-1957 and approximately nine years of independence with only five-and-a-half years as a republic, the CPP under Nkrumah founded three universities, hundreds of public schools and provided scholarships to Ghanaian students to study abroad as well as other Africans to matriculate inside of Ghana itself.

This level of literary and scholastic achievements was illustrated in the CPP press. Outstanding journalists and writers from Ghana and other states were published on a daily basis. One leading woman journalist and CPP operative was Mabel Ellen Dove. She was one of the most interesting figures within the upper echelons of the party since Dove had once been married to UGCC leader J.B. Danquah, who later became a staunch opponent of Nkrumah and the CPP after the split in June 1949.

Dove wrote extensively on issues involving national liberation, Pan-Africanism and anti-imperialism. On the tenth anniversary of the beginning of the Positive Action campaign, a general strike called by the CPP on January 8, 1950, which was so effective that it landed Nkrumah in prison for a year, Dove published an article in the Evening News entitled "Africanism unto Calvary."

She describes the party rally to commemorate the anniversary saying "A sea of eager, dedicated faces, thousands upon thousands of them in the historic Arena. Men, women and children, individuals, voluntary organizations, trade unions, benevolent societies and still they come. On the tree tops they hang precariously on the branches, on the top of the 'mammy lorries', there is no more room in the Arena but thousands are still thronging outside waiting to hear the Leader." (Evening News, Jan. 12, 1960, p. 3)

The article continues observing "On the wooden platform could be seen the old fighting warriors still consistent, still loyal to the Leader in the fight for the 'redemption and liberation' of all Africa. The

Leader is calling on them once more to rededicate themselves to the economic and social reconstruction of Ghana and the coming together of the nations of Africa—Africanism the new ideology. Other peoples and races of the past had to creep, walk and run but as the Leader said for us 'The Time is Short'. The African has to run and leap and to move with extended hand towards his brother. Pettiness, envy, selfishness, greed, vanity, vindictiveness, hatred, malice, cannot be indulged in by the African, dedicated to the service of his country and his continent, Mother Africa."

In this same essay Dove asks "What is Africanism? Africanism is the belief by patriots in the new and emerging nations of Africa that this great continent of Africa is made by the almighty the Creator of all men for Africans and that Africans should live in this continent in dignity and pride, to work and enjoy the fruits of their labor and that the natural resources of this great continent should be exploited for the progress of the Africans and that they should walk with uplifted heads and a song in his heart in any part of Africa….. Despite all the set-backs in the way of the African he has shown again and again that brutality, auto-suggestions, exploitation, poverty, disease and illiteracy have not been able to destroy him physically and spiritually and when imperialism is destroyed Africans may produce the first super-men…. The supposed Christians of Western civilization have to throw away their cant, humbug, hypocrisy and sheer malevolent brutality in Africa or take the consequences of their inhumanity to man. Africanism is the new religion to be practiced and propagated by the patriots of the new and emerging nations of Africa even unto Calvary."

The general atmosphere surrounding the Conference of the Women of Africa and African Descent gathering was Pan-Africanist and internationalist. Ghana's First Lady Madam Fathia Nkrumah, who was born in the North African state of Egypt, greeted delegations from her home country as well as neighboring Tunisia. Panel discussions at the conference featured presentations by Cudjoe and

Armarteifio sharing platforms with women from other regions of the continent.

Nkrumah during his speech at Baden Powell Memorial Hall stressed: "I repeat what I have many times stated before, that the independence of Ghana is meaningless, unless it is linked up with the total liberation of Africa. Therefore, the struggle in Ghana still continues and our women are still combatant troops. I would like to take this opportunity today to pay tribute to them.
This Conference, organized by the Ghana Women's Movement which represents all women's groups in the country, must ask the questions: why the women of South Africa must be in possession of passes in order to go about their ordinary business? Why apartheid overlords should shoot down defenseless women and children in their God-given land in order to maintain white supremacy? Why is Africa an extension of Europe? Why Algeria, a country on African soil, should be claimed as French? Why South Africa should flout the authority of the United Nations over South-West Africa? What part can the women of Africa and of African descent play in the struggle for African emancipation? What part can the women of African descent anywhere in the world play in the struggle for African emancipation? You must ask these questions not by word of mouth, but by action — by positive action, which is the only language understood by the detractors of African freedom."

Less than two weeks prior to the Conference of the Women of Africa and African Descent the CPP women's section attended a party at the presidential office in Flagstaff House. Nkrumah hosted ten representatives from each of the eight regions of Ghana. Officers of the CPP national headquarters were in attendance as well. (Evening News, July 8, 1960)

On a personal level Nkrumah was very close to his mother and took good care of her during his tenure in political office. Members of the National Association of Socialist Students Organizations (NASSO) paid tribute to Madam Nyaniba, the mother of Nkrumah, at a gathering in Accra. According to the January 25, 1960 edition of the Evening News on its front page it notes that Madam Nyaniba told the students "Anything that has not the blessing of God will not succeed. The Voice of the People is the Voice of God." Madame Nyaniba encouraged the youth to be honest and sincere in their dealings with their comrades and all their endeavors.

Women and Historical Pan-Africanism

The CPP and the Ghana government were committed to the realization of a United States of Africa under socialism. The party viewed the struggle for national liberation as an initial step towards continental unity and non-capitalist development. The editorial policy of the party press was to provide unconditional political and ideological support to the national liberation movements still fighting to throw off the yoke of colonialism along with those anti-imperialist states such as Guinea-Conakry under President Ahmed Sekou Toure and Malian President Modibo Kieta. In 1960 the Ghana-Guinea-Mali Union was formed pledging to work towards political and economic integration.

Mabel Dove wrote on January 8, 1960, the tenth anniversary of the Positive Action Campaign of 1950, about the plight of Nyasaland African National Congress leader Dr. Hastings Banda who was incarcerated by the British at the time. Dove noted that Dr. Banda said when he was sentenced to prison that it fulfilled one of his ambitions "to be put in prison for my people like Dr. Kwame Nkrumah." (Evening News, Jan. 8, p. 8)

She continued in this same report emphasizing "Imperialism is actually desperate in Central Africa and the arrest of African leaders like Dr. Banda provide evidence of frenzy and uneasiness which have gripped the arbitrary rulers in their murderous campaign which they seek to cloak in their imaginary 'discovery' of a 'Slaughter plot'."

On the same page of this issue of the Evening News, Dove pens another article entitled "Free Jomo Kenyatta", the Kenyan nationalist leader who was imprisoned for his efforts aimed at winning independence for this East African settler colony. Kenyatta had worked with Nkrumah at the Fifth Pan-African Congress held in Manchester, England in October 1945.

Dove said: "The trend today is the propaganda that white settlers in Africa are Africans. The white in any part of Africa is not an African and he can never be an African by any stretch of the imagination and the dishonorable action of imperialism of fostering these settlers on Africans and trying willy-nilly to place political power in their hands so that they become another South African horror on the Continent is the danger that is facing Africa and Africans today."

This same article about Kenyatta goes on stressing: "The physical and mental vigor of the African has saved him from total extermination despite the slave trade, the deadly weapons and the inhuman atrocities against his soul and body, and now with his eyes on the goal of freedom, arrogant and unrepentant imperialism with her greedy eyes on the natural resources of Africa, is still spending sleepless nights and traveling great distances to create by hook or crook White Domination in Black Africa."

During 1960, despite the proclamations of it being "The Year of Africa", a serious crisis would erupt which would create divisions within the body politic of the newly emergent continental states. Patrice Lumumba, who had gained considerable support from Ghana while in attendance at the First All-African People's Conference in Accra in December 1958, was soon arrested after returning to the Belgian Congo in January 1959.

Lumumba was tortured while in detention and the colonialists sought to exclude him from political negotiations that took place in the aftermath of a national rebellion in early 1959. His release and participation in the discussions surrounding the proposed independence of the vast mineral-rich Central African state would enhance his reputation as a Nationalist and Pan-Africanist across Africa and the world.

As the leader of the Congolese National Movement (MNC), Lumumba would garner the largest bloc of votes winning him the prime minister position at the time of independence on June 30, 1960. Nonetheless, imperialism was staunchly opposed to the program of the MNC-Lumumba and worked incessantly to undermine the liberation process.

The Congolese prime minister faced a mutiny of the para-military Force Publique in the immediate aftermath of the declaration of independence. Lumumba would appeal to other African states such as Ghana and Guinea to provide assistance in the stabilization of the country. Eventually he requested the intervention of the United Nations then under Secretary General Dag Hammarskjold.

When the UN troops entered Leopoldville, the Congolese capital, they objectively worked in the interests of imperialism. A contingent of Ghana troops were deployed as part of the UN force under the command of British Major General Henry Templer Alexander. The outcome of this project would be disastrous. Nkrumah perceived the performance of Alexander as defying the foreign policy objectives of the Ghana government and eventually dismissed him from his post by 1961.

Lumumba was overthrown in a military coup backed up by the UN peacekeeping forces. He later escaped from Leopoldville to join his supporters in the East of the country where they had sought to establish a genuine people's republic. However, Lumumba was tracked and captured by the Belgian and other imperialist military forces that were still operating inside the country delivering him to the reactionary political puppet functionaries working on behalf of Moise Tshome, the secessionist of the Katanga province, and Joseph Mobuto, who at the aegis of the Central Intelligence Agency

(CIA) and other Western interests, was placed in power for the express purpose of liquidating Lumumba and his MNC party.

Since the time of the death of Lumumba and his comrades, various operative of the CIA, the U.S. State Department, the Belgian colonial authorities and the British intelligence services (MI6) have admitted to the plot to kill Lumumba. Initial efforts were made to poison the Congolese leader which failed. The kidnapping place Lumumba at the mercy of his enemies and he was reportedly assassinated on January 17, 1961 in Elizabethville in Congo.

The assassination of Lumumba prompted outrage throughout the African continent and the world. In the U.S. at the UN world headquarters, a group of African Americans, led by women, disrupted a session chaired by American envoy Adlai Stevenson.

Lumumba's assassination was ordered by the National Security Council of the U.S. under the administration of retired Gen. Dwight D. Eisenhower. Several days later, the administration of President John F. Kennedy took office and continued the same policy towards Congo. (See The Congo Cables: The Cold War in Africa From Eisenhower to Kennedy, by Madeleine G. Kalb, 1982))

The Kennedy presidency presented a false image of support for African independence. This in part derived from a Cold War strategy of outmaneuvering the Union of Soviet Socialist Republics (USSR) and the People's Republic of China and their foreign policies that categorically rejected colonialism and imperialism in defense of the African people's inherent right to self-determination and national independence.

Kennedy while serving a term in the U.S. Senate from 1954-1960 established a sub-committee on African affairs. This was part of a broader effort to win over not only the emergent African states but also the African American electorate by giving the appearance that he was sympathetic to their interests in the U.S. as well.

Nkrumah came to the U.S. on March 8, 1961 for consultations with Kennedy. Nevertheless, the damage had already been done with the assassination of Lumumba and the derailing of the Congolese Revolution and its Pan-Africanist leanings.

A U.S. State Department synopsis of the meeting between the Ghana delegation and Kennedy administration officials said: "In summary, the two Presidents found themselves in agreement on three principal points on the Congo, (1) removal of Belgian military and para-military personnel, (2) neutralization of Congolese military forces and insulation of the Congo against outside influences and military supplies, and (3) freedom for the Congolese to work out their own political development. On the last point the Secretary called attention to our own history to illustrate the importance we attach to the principle that government must be based on consent of the governed. In addition to examples from our early history he cited our important role in assisting Indonesian independence and President Roosevelt's heavy pressure on Churchill, even while we were allies in a world war, in regard to India. There should be no doubt, therefore, in any reasonable mind, that the U.S. would always be basically, and in the long run effectively, on the side of anti-colonialism and independence, whether the problem is Portugal and Angola or France and Algeria or any other." (U.S. State Dept. archives on Africa policy from 1961-1963)

According to this same declassified report from the State Department: "President Nkrumah exhibited no desire to talk about U.S. - Ghana bilateral relations and at one point turned off the Secretary's attempt to bring up the Volta project. President Nkrumah did, however, make the point that the U.S. should broaden its view of Africa and look at the continent as a whole, a subject which he said he had raised when he was here in 1958. The President (Kennedy) took this opportunity to explain the difficulties we face in Africa. He cited the resentment inspired in ``colonialist" circles by Governor (G.M.) Williams' (Undersecretary for African

Affairs) alleged statement on ``Africa for the Africans" in Nairobi and pointed out that despite this, Governor Williams had been given an unfriendly reception by the press in Lagos. The President (Kennedy) also expressed his surprise and puzzlement over receipt of a recent personal message from Sekou Toure accusing him of complicity in Lumumba's murder. President Nkrumah seemed sympathetic but offered no very specific advice or comment."

Responses to the Congo crisis would divide the newly-independent African states into two separate political camps: the Casablanca Group characterized by its anti-imperialism and Pan-Africanism and the Monrovia Group, which was perceived as more favorable to the U.S. and other colonial and neo-colonial states. Although Nkrumah sought to maintain cordial relations with the Kennedy administration, the overall domestic and foreign policy orientation of the CPP government was anti-capitalist and anti-imperialist. (See Nkrumah's Challenge of the Congo, 1967 and Revolutionary Path, 1973)

These developments further aggravated relations between Accra and Washington. Nkrumah's government would soon move closer to the USSR, the COMECON sector in Eastern Europe and the People's Republic of China. Pressure would escalate against the CPP through the machinations of the CIA and the State Department.

From August 1962 to early 1964, a series of assassination attempts against Nkrumah and mass killings of Ghanaians were blamed on outside interests. The attack on Nkrumah at Kulungugu in the North of the country near the border with Upper Volta set off a massive purge within the CPP.

Leading figures in what was considered the left-wing of the party were accused of being behind the plot. Adamafio and others were put on trial and later acquitted by the Ghana courts. Nkrumah objected to the not-guilty verdicts and dismissed the judges setting up another proceeding that found many of the accused culpable, landing them in prison.

In early January 1964, yet another assassination attempt against Nkrumah by a guard at Flagstaff House increased the atmosphere of siege against the CPP government. A national referendum on making Ghana a one-party state was held solidifying the Revolution as being on a firm socialist path with the central foreign policy objective being the realization of a United States of Africa.

Nkrumah had welcomed several hundred African Americans to Ghana where many played important roles within his government. In October 1961, Dr. W.E.B. Du Bois and Shirley Graham Du Bois would locate in Ghana eventually taking up citizenship in the country.

Dr. Du Bois was appointed as the Director of the Encyclopedia Africana Project which was designed to develop a comprehensive history and political economy of the African people. Shirley Graham Du Bois was assigned to develop a national television network based in Ghana, the first of its kind envisioned on the African continent. Both of the Du Bois' were well-known leftist and Pan-Africanists. The Du Bois' were both members of the Communist Party of the U.S. and had traveled extensively throughout the USSR, China and other Socialist states.

During the Cold War hysteria of the late 1940s and 1950s inside the U.S., Dr. Du Bois in 1951, was indicted by the federal government for allegedly being an agent of a foreign belief system simply because he was an advocate of peace with the Socialist camp. The American government's case collapsed under the absurdity of the charges. However, the couple had their passports seized and were not allowed to travel outside the U.S. during the period of 1950-1958.

A host of other activists were targeted as well including Paul Robeson and Dr. William Alphaeus Hunton, Jr., who with Dr. Du Bois and Robeson headed the Council on African Affairs (CAA). Nkrumah had participated in CAA activities during the mid-1940s when he was a student in the U.S.

When their passports were re-issued in 1958, the Du Bois' embarked upon a world tour of the Socialist countries and other states in Europe. Graham Du Bois visited Ghana in December 1958 for the All-African People's Conference where she delivered an address written by Dr. Du Bois, who was not able to attend at that time.

This speech was entitled "The Future of All-Africa Lies in Socialism." It said in part, in regard to which direction the continent would move as it relates to social development, asking: "Which way shall Africa go? First, I would emphasize the fact that today Africa has no choice between private Capitalism and Socialism. The whole world, including Capitalist countries, is moving towards Socialism, inevitably, inexorably. You can choose between blocs of military alliances, you can choose between groups of political unions, you cannot choose between Socialism and private Capitalism, because private ownership of capital is doomed."

The Du Bois' continued saying to the 62 national liberation movements assembled in Accra: "But what is Socialism? It is disciplined economy and political organization in which the first duty of a citizen is to serve the state; and the state is not a selected aristocracy, or a group of self-seeking oligarchs who have seized wealth and power. No! The mass of workers with hand and brain are the ones whose collective destiny is the chief object of all effort. Here then, my brothers, you face your great decision: Will you for temporary advantage--for automobiles, refrigerators and Paris gowns--spend your income in paying interest on borrowed funds, or will you sacrifice present comfort and the chance to shine before your neighbors in order to educate your children, develop such industry as best serves the great mass of people and makes your country strong in ability, self-support and self-defense? Such union of effort for strength calls for sacrifice and self-denial, while the capital offered you at high price by the colonial powers like France, Britain, Holland, Belgium and the United States, will prolong fatal colonial imperialism, from which you have suffered slavery, serfdom and colonialism."

Of course there were other African Americans and Caribbean Africans who played a role in the Ghana Revolution and Pan-Africanism. People such as Vicki Garvin, a longtime Communist and activist was in Ghana at the time. Maya Angelou, the writer and dancer taught school in Ghana and worked in defense of the Nkrumah project. Alice Windom, another African American woman was in Ghana participating in national development efforts.

All of these women worked with Julian Mayfield, the novelist and journalist, who after fleeing the U.S. in 1961 amid the Federal Bureau of Investigation's (FBI) hunt for Monroe, North Carolina organizer and former local NAACP leaders Robert F. Williams and Mabel Williams, relocated in Ghana becoming a publicity secretary for the parliament and editor of African Review, a journal of Pan-Africanist thought.

Julian Mayfield along with Windom, Angelou and Garvin would host the two visits of Malcolm X to Ghana during 1964. Malcolm X mentioned in his final speech in Detroit that the first chapter of the Organization of Afro-American Unity (OAAU) was formed in Ghana. This was initiated after he left of the Nation of Islam in 1964 being patterned in part on the Organization of African Unity (OAU), founded in May 1963 in Addis Ababa, Ethiopia with 32 member-states.

Socialism, Women's Liberation and the Struggle for World Peace

Revolutionary socialists throughout the period from the late 19<sup>th</sup> century to the middle of the 20<sup>th</sup>, viewed gender oppression and discrimination as integral to the class struggle against capitalism and imperialism. This was articulated by Clara Zetkin, a German woman who was a leading member of the Social Democratic Party (SPD).

In her speech delivered to the Party Congress in Berlin on October 16, 1896, she drew a clear distinction between bourgeois and socialist feminism. Zetkin said during the address that the capitalist ruling class had no fundamental opposition to bourgeois feminism since it did not challenge the economic status of the owners of the means of production.

The speech was entitled "Only in Conjunction with the Proletarian Woman Will Socialism Be Victorious." In this contribution Zetkin maintains: "The liberation struggle of the proletarian woman cannot be similar to the struggle that the bourgeois woman wages against the male of her class. On the contrary, it must be a joint struggle with the male of her class against the entire class of capitalists. She does not need to fight against the men of her class in order to tear down the barriers which have been raised against her participation in the free competition of the market place. Capitalism's need to exploit and the development of the modern mode of production totally relieves her of having to fight such a struggle. On the contrary, new barriers need to be erected against the exploitation of the proletarian woman. Her rights as wife and mother need to be restored and permanently secured. Her final aim is not the free competition with the man, but the achievement of the political rule of the proletariat. The proletarian woman fights hand in hand with the man of her class against capitalist society. To be sure, she also agrees with the demands of the bourgeois women's movement, but she regards the fulfillment of these demands simply as a means to enable that movement to enter the battle, equipped with the same weapons, alongside the proletariat."

During her tenure in the SPD, Zetkin, along with Rosa Luxemburg, who was a close friend and collaborator, were central figures in the left wing of the party. As a result of political developments inside the party, a debate on revisionism erupted at the turn of the 20th century. Zetkin and Luxemburg together waged an ideological and political struggle against the dominant theoretician Eduard Bernstein.

Zetkin wrote extensively on women's affairs particularly in regard to the movement to end discrimination and the acquisition of women's suffrage. Her efforts assisted in the development of the social-democratic women's movement in Germany.  In the years from 1891 to 1917 Zetkin edited the SPD women's publication Die Gleichheit (Equality). Later in 1907 she took over the leadership of the recently-created "Women's Office" for the SPD. Zetkin is credited with creating the first "International Women's Day" on March 8, 1911, having launched the project in Copenhagen, in what later became the Ungdomshuset.

In the aftermath of the Socialist revolution in Russia and the formation of the USSR, the role of women in society was transformed dramatically. Resolutions were passed against institutional discrimination based upon gender and women participated fully in various aspects of Soviet society.

These revolutions would occur in Korea, Vietnam, China, Yugoslavia and Albania during the years following World War II. The international division of political and economic power was growing pitting the Socialist states, the national liberations movements against colonialism and imperialism based in the capitalist countries of Western Europe and North America. The wars waged against the Democratic People's Republic of Korea (DPRK), North Vietnam and the People's Republic of China were also aimed at arresting and redirecting the national liberation movements many of whom were influenced by anti-capitalist ideas.

One key element in the domination of U.S. imperialism in the Post World War II period related to the maintenance of American territory during the fighting and the utilization of the Atomic bomb against Japan in August 1945. The was clearly an act of aggression directed not just against the already defeated Japanese ruling class but its broader purpose was to put the Socialist countries and liberation movements on notice that the number one imperialist state was more than willing to reign down death and destruction at unprecedented levels.

In the period leading up to the Conference of the Women of Africa and African Descent in July 1960, the Ghana government was launching its own campaign against the plans of the French government under Charles De Gaulle to test an atomic weapon in the Sahara on Algerian territory. These plans were taking place in congruity with the armed and mass struggle by the Algerian people for independence.

The Ghana Evening News took a strong position in solidarity with the movement to prevent the test from occurring. In the January 4, 1960 issue of the state-run paper there was a letter to the editor written by O'ba Owusu-Akyem, a Stone Contractor from Tema, who expressed support for a Protest Team seeking to travel to the area of the proposed test.

Owusu-Akyem said in the letter that "by their patriotic action, stubborn France must know that the whole of the continent of Africa is deadly against that terrible test and it must be stopped in the precious name of humanity."

In another letter to the editor published in the same issue of the Evening News by Kwasi-Kwadjo of Asafo, it says: "I have just heard that the French authorities have arrested the members of the Sahara Protest Team who are going peacefully about their duty in the service of humanity…. Africa has spoken against this Sahara test and the world has supported Africa in her protest and it is left to France to show a keen sense of sympathy and respect for mankind."

CPP journalist Mabel Dove in her article based upon an interview with French pacifist Pierre Martin, who was staging an ongoing protest against the pending weapons test outside Paris' embassy at Ghana House in Accra, outlined the solidarity of the Nkrumah government with the hunger strike against the utilization of these weapons in Africa. Dove quoted Martin as saying: "There are two embassies in Ghana today, I Pierre Martin. I am the ambassador representing the people of France and the embassy on the fifth floor of Ghana House represents French Officialdom." (Evening News, Jan. 4, 1960)

Dove asked Martin did he think his fast could stop the test. Martin responded saying "If General de Gaulle so desires, the atom test in the Sahara could be stopped."

This article goes on to report: "In the hands of Pierre Martin was a pamphlet. I (Dove) glanced through it and I will give you the details of the findings of a group of scientists in the Atomic Energy Commission of the United States of America. 'As surely as a bomb is exploded thousands of persons will fall sick and will die in some part of the world. Carbon 14 the most menacing radioactive substances, is a menace because it lives so long, 8,000 years. Up to the moment biological peril to man of Carbon 14 has been responsible for '100,000 major defectives, physical as well as psychological; 380,000 still born children and of infant mortality and 900,000 cases of embryonic and neo-natal deaths. And yet despite all these horrors, France proposed to test in the middle of the African continent, an absolute bomb of no scientific value because according to Christian France, the most powerful countries are those who have these diabolical weapons and France believes that by endangering the lives of 200 million Africans she will become a powerful nation."

Later on January 15, 1960, the Evening News reported on the mobilization of the Ghana Women's movement in opposition to the French atomic test. An article on the front page of the paper entitled "Women Federation Presents G21 Cheque", reported on the contribution to the Ghana Council for Nuclear Disarmament.

The article reveals that Mr. E.C. Quaye, Chairman of the Ghana Council for Nuclear Disarmament, received the gift from a three-member delegation of the Ghana Federation of Women. These women were Mrs. A.M. Akiwumi, the National President, Dr. Evelyn Armateifio, the General Secretary, and Mrs. Elsie Ofuatey Cudjoe, an executive member of the Federation.

This presentation of funds was held at the Accra Municipal Council and Dr. Armateifio "told the Evening News that at the Federation's annual conference held at Keta, it was unanimously decided to make financial contributions to help the Sahara Protest Team. To this end the conference resolved to organize rallies to launch an appeal for funds. Yesterday's contribution was proceeds from rallies held at Peki and Half Asini."

Some ten days later the Second All-African People's Conference was convened in Tunisia which immediately went on record as condemning the proposed nuclear test by the French government. On the first day of the gathering there was a rally held in opposition to the French test which was sponsored by the ruling Neo-Destour party. The Evening News of January 25, 1960 said: "The underlying theme of the conference is 'Freedom and Unity' and how to complete Africa's independence and weld it into one unit grouping all 230 million Africans. Delegates from more than 30 nations are taking part in the conference." (p. 6)

Despite this widespread sentiment in Africa against the French test in the Sahara, it was carried out on February 13, 1960. This was its first atomic bomb and was known as Blue Jerboa. In 2014, declassified documents indicated that radiation emanating from the operation in the Algerian desert extended much further than what was stated at the time.

The Digital Journal noted in an article by Anne Sewell that: "In fact, the radiation fallout is likely to have reached as far as the southern coast of Spain as well as Sicily and Sardinia in Italy, within just 13 days of the blast. The French daily newspaper Le Parisien published the military papers on February 14, 2014."

Le Parisien emphasized: "The military recognizes that in some places the safety standards have been widely exceeded: Arak near Tamanrasset, where the water was highly contaminated but also in the Chadian capital N'Djamena….. The documents also show that dangerous levels of iodine-131 and caesium-137 were discovered in Chad's capital, N'Djamena, along with Arak, near Tamanrasset in southern Algeria. However, it is impossible to tell the exact levels involved. Everyone knows today that these radioactive elements cause cancers or cardio-vascular diseases."

These documents illustrated there were four atomic bomb tests in the Sahara prior to the independence of Algeria in 1962. In addition, the declassified materials indicate there were 13 additional tests in the post-independence period until 1966 when they were halted. France then resumed atomic testing in Polynesian territory in 1970.

The Digitial Journal report says: "Around 150,000 people living within the blast zone are reportedly yet to be compensated by 2014. On top of this, some illnesses suffered by French soldiers have been established to be the result of exposure to radiation from the blasts. The weapon was detonated atop a 105 meter tower near Reganne, Algeria. According to a description video, the test was a pure fission device with a plutonium core and a one-point initiated implosion system."

Ghana's criticism of France and other imperialist states in the early 1960s created animosity towards the Nkrumah government by the most powerful colonial and neo-colonial states. The concerns of the western governments and their allies in the region were fueled by the industrial and modernization program of the CPP. The opening of three universities: Legon, Cape Coast and Kwame Nkrumah University of Science and Technology in Kumasi, led to the rapid advancement of the technical and literary capacity of the newly-independent nation.

Nkrumah and the CPP through its coterie of journalists, propagandists, diplomats, educators and organizers welded tremendous influence among the masses of workers, youth and farmers throughout Africa. This dissemination of the Pan-Africanist and Socialist ideology of the party impacted African Americans and other diasporic communities in the Caribbean, Latin America and Western Europe. After 1961, Ghana moved even closer towards the Soviet Union, China, Cuba and other Socialist countries. With the CPP press being openly anti-capitalist in its orientation and editorial policy prompted the accelerated plans aimed at undermining the Nkrumaist project and the African Revolution as a whole.

After the deadly CIA-backed attacks between 1962 and 1964, the CPP government still remained intact. The Volta River Dam being constructed by Kaiser Aluminum was designed to provide the first stage of a rapid industrialization scheme which was spelled out in the party document "The Seven Year Plan for Work and Happiness."

Therefore by February 7, 1964, just over a month after yet another assassination attempt against President Nkrumah, Shirley Graham Du Bois, then the Director of Ghana National Television, could write to her lawyer Bernard Jaffe in New York City from Accra saying: "I didn't expect things to 'burst' with such violence, but I am sure you have read enough in your newspaper and heard on the radio that relations between the U.S. and Ghana are 'strained.' I heard on BBC last night that the U.S. Ambassador had been recalled from here as a token of 'displeasure'. I have not yet heard whether or not Ghana's Ambassador has been recalled from Washington. I do not know what will happen. I do know that had the citizens of a small country, a few years ago, tore down the U.S. flag as was done here Tuesday, gun boats would already be in that small country's harbor..... For several days the newspapers here really have out-done themselves. Somebody is really fed up!" (Correspondence in files stored at the Univ. of Mass. at Amherst)

Graham Du Bois continues in this same letter to Jaffe noting: "For some time evidence has been piling up which the Ghanaians accept as proof that the last attempt on the President's life was engineered by the CIA. A number of persons have been arrested. Last week five American teachers at the University were ordered to leave the country. And this week came the two huge demonstrations around the U.S. Embassy. There is no longer any secrecy about any of this. All I can say is the African Revolution is rolling along. And revolutions are never exactly joy rides."

Nonetheless, the work of the CPP continued at full speed. Graham Du Bois' correspondence with Jaffe reports on her trip to Japan in March 1964 where the government in Tokyo was providing considerable technical support for the development of Ghana National Television. She said in a letter dated March 18 that she "came back from Japan fired with an IDEA. I want to start Ghana Television in color! After what I have seen in Japan, after what I have learned, after the contacts I made, etc. etc. etc. I KNOW IT CAN BE DONE."

Describing her responsibilities as a major figure in the CPP government, Graham Du Bois wrote in her letter to Jaffe that she was the head of an eight million dollar project to establish this television network. That she has "the responsibility to plan, administer, recruit workers, train workers here and decide who shall be sent away for special training, check equipment, choose equipment, buy equipment, watch over the final construction of buildings which is costing the government over three million pounds. The British and Canadians are already in on this project. The fact that I am now going to bring the Japanese in on it is going to be explosive news."

The Ghana National Television Director tells Jaffe of her exceptional reception in Japan. Graham Du Bois says she was somewhat of a "sensation" in Japan. She was featured on Japanese television twice and in an extended interview over radio which was broadcast to many regions of the world. "The people were wonderful to me and I certainly did tie down their interest in Ghana!"

In addition to being Director of National Television, Graham Du Bois was also a member of the National Planning Commission and the Board of Directors of the State Publishing House, which opened during the latter months of 1964. Other responsibilities included serving on the Publicity Committee of the Secretariat for the Third Organization of African Unity Summit which took place in Accra in October 1965. She told Jaffe that "I am called upon at all hours of the day and night to be advisor, sympathizer, companion, relaxation and stimulation and sources of information, to fill a Consuming Fire of Demands, Visions and Needs!" (Letter to Jaffe, August 16, 1964)

However, by February 21, 1965, Graham Du Bois explains in another letter to Jaffe that the situation in Ghana is becoming complicated due to U.S. interference. She places these problems within the context of the broader instability and Cold War exigencies across the world. Although Ghana appears to be a place of refuge for African and African American freedom fighters with the rapid process of development, the independent character of the CPP government has made it a target of U.S. imperialism.

In response to the Pan-Africanist and Socialist orientation of the Nkrumah administration, Graham Du Bois asks: "So what happens? Attempts at assassination fail! Attempts at stirring up internal dissension fail! We keep moving forward. So now the World

Marketers close in! They are trying to strangle our economy, cut off our trade, freeze certain foreign exchange, while, at the same time, choke us with foreign goods. Nkrumah answers by refusing to release precious cocoa, imposing rigid import restrictions and telling us we must Do Without until new adjustments can be made with socialist countries! It will work. Nobody is going to starve, but new, industrial projects such as TELEVISION have been hard hit. Television must import everything in the line of equipment and working materials. And here we are—in the last quarter, ready to make final for beginning and unable to get final essentials for our work. I must 'hold the line' and 'keep the high morals and spirits of my workers', continue with everything it is possible to do—and there is much to do—and radiate assurance that everything will be all right!... All the forces of history are on our side. It would be ridiculous to treat it as such. But this kind of situation produces daily a hundred irritating stresses and strains, uncertainties and embarrassments."

Some four months later, Graham Du Bois records the escalating pressure from the imperialist countries. She notes in her letter to Jaffe on June 17, 1965, that despite the fact of being "shaken, weary and bloody, our heads are 'unbowed' and we are now marching forward on firm ground which rises to a higher level than ever before."

The Ghana National Television Director reports that: "Every possible economic and political device has been used by enemies to prevent the holding of the Third African Summit Conference in Accra next September as scheduled. But last week at the Foreign Ministers Conference in Lagos, Nigeria, the last obstacle was swept away and by unanimous agreement the Conference will be held."

This OAU Summit held in Accra during October 1965 was the last before the overthrow of the CPP that following February 24, 1966. The summit took place in a brand new conference center that was magnificent in its splendor. American novelist Truman Nelson was interested in traveling to Ghana as an incentive for a writing project on the life of Dr. Du Bois. He arrived during the period leading up to the OAU Summit in Accra and Graham Du Bois felt that the writer was roundly impressed with the political and economic progress being made in Ghana.

In a letter to Jaffe dated November 21, 1965, she says: "In spite of all we tell them, Americans do come to Ghana with certain preconceived ideas. Now, as you know, Ghana is a big surprise when you see it for the first time under normal conditions."

Of the OAU gathering, Graham Du Bois stressed: "There is nothing like our Summit Compound in the world. I have seen the United Nations building in New York, the Conference Chambers in Geneva and conference building in many world capitals. But ours is uniquely distinctive! The first time Truman entered the Conference Hall (the Compound is composed of three buildings) he said in a stunned voice, 'But this is better than the UN Building!'"

Nelson was taken to the site of the Akosombo Dam on the Volta River which was scheduled for a grand opening by January 1966. He was able to return to Accra with President Nkrumah in the state helicopter.

The Director felt the staff of the Ghana network was highly professional in handling the event. Graham Du Bois said: "In addition to pieces which we had collected from every independent African country and presented to the edification of the Heads of State and their delegations, we covered all open sessions of the Conference live. This meant that some of my teams—with me— were often on duty from early morning of one day until two or three a.m. the next morning. We had both Josephine Baker from Paris and Mariam Makeba from New York as 'special entertainers'."

Nevertheless, the OAU Summit in Ghana attracted the ire of the U.S. and other imperialist governments. Many of the Heads of State failed to attend sending envoys instead. The burgeoning crisis over the imminent "Unilateral Declaration of Independence" by the British settler-colony in Rhodesia (Zimbabwe) was the focus of the Summit along with the Nkrumaist objective of the formation of a United States Africa encompassing an "All-African Military High Command", political and economic integration and the consequent breaking down of borders and the adoption of a single currency.

By November 11, the UDI had been adopted in Rhodesia leading to United Nations and Commonwealth sanctions against the settler-colony. However, Nkrumah demanded the total isolation of the settlers even up to the point of military intervention. The CPP government in line with the resolutions passed at the OAU Summit in Accra broke diplomatic relations with Britain along with nine of the 39 governments who were then member-states.

These other OAU member countries included Algeria, Congo-Brazzaville, Guinea-Conakry, Mauritania, Mali, Tanzania, Sudan and the United Arab Republic (Egypt). After the coup against the CPP in February 1966, a number of these states gradually re-established relations by 1967-1968. (Modern Diplomacy, R. P. Barston, Fourth Edition, 2013)

In a December 12, 1965 letter from Graham Du Bois to Jaffe, she remarks: "you can imagine the general state of our nerves here in Ghana. Thursday evening's television showed me leading all my television workers to sign up for our Voluntary Peoples Militia.

The coup against Nkrumah was engineered by the CIA and the U.S. State Department on February 24, 1966. Acting on behalf of imperialist interests, a group of lower-ranking military officers and police waited until the President left the country on a mission aimed at ending the U.S. war against Vietnam. He stopped over in Peking in route to Hanoi and was informed by Premier Chou En Lai that a coup had taken place in Ghana. Nkrumah acted with disbelief while the Chinese Communist leader told him that these are things which occur during the course of the revolutionary struggle. (See Dark Days in Ghana, Kwame Nkrumah, 1968)

Conclusion: Pan-Africanism or Neo-Colonialism in the 21st Century?

"Operation Cold Chop" was conducted with extreme swiftness and efficiency during the early morning hours of February 24, 1966. The top leaders within the Ghana military who did not support the coup were either assassinated or placed in detention. Hundreds of CPP officials were arrested and taken immediately to prison.

At the same time, those held in detention by the CPP government were released in order to lead demonstrations in support of the coup through the streets of Accra. Thousands of party members, functionaries, propagandists and journalists were terminated from their positions. CPP books and other Socialist literature were burned in the streets in an orgy of counter-revolutionary fervor in genuflection to the imperialist countries.

Industrial projects, educational programs and party publications were shut down under the guise that they were not profitable and a liability to the Ghana state. Show trials in the form of tribunals against corruption were held for national and international consumption in an effort to rationalize and justify the unconstitutional removal of an elected and recognized government.

No real appreciation of the challenges facing a post-colonial African state was taken into consideration in developing the narrative against the Nkrumah-CPP era. With Ghana being a former slave and colonial territory, the structural obstacles to national integration and economic development were formidable by the time the country embarked upon an independent path.

During the early to mid-1960s when Nkrumah was in power under the Republic system, approximately 60 percent of the labor force was involved in agricultural production. In 1961, manufacturing generated a mere two percent of the overall gross domestic product. Agricultural production of manioc, maize, yams, plantain, taro, millets, and sorghums, and rice accounted for 80 percent or more of the caloric consumption. (See Ann Seidman and Marvin P. Miracle, State Farms in Ghana, 1968)

Nonetheless, another impediment in evaluating any form of progress by developing states is related to the limited nature of data which can hamper any substantial assessment and analysis of what is considered success and failure as it relates to post-colonial development projects particularly those that sought to shift production towards state-owned enterprises in the agricultural sector.

As the process of evaluation of Ghana's largest agricultural export, cocoa, analysts suggest that the data available is much more reliable. The UN Food and Agricultural Organization (FAO) in its statistical reports on the production of cocoa indicate that there was an increase of 70 percent in the aftermath of World War II. However, there was a decline in cocoa prices on the international market in the early 1960s and consequently foreign exchange earned by Ghana remained stagnant.

By 1961 as the development policies enacted by the Nkrumah government shifted more towards the models in operation in the Soviet Union, China and Eastern European socialist states, the First Republic sought to invest more resources into the creation of state farms. Although the British colonial authorities had established state enterprise projects in agricultural as early as 1950, more of these efforts were undertaken under the Seven-Year Development Plan for 1963-64 to 1969-70, which was designed to institutionalize Socialist economic production inside the Ghana.

Under the rubric of the State Farms Corporation (SFC), the Nkrumah government set about to transform agricultural production with the expressed intent to reduce reliance on the importation of both food stuffs and other commodities. These SFC initiated projects would also be utilized in supplying materials for industrial production as well.

The Development program issued in 1962 says: "The farming plan for the State Farms Corporation during the next seven years envisages heavy concentration on cereal and basic crops especially to meet demand in the rapidly expanding urban areas and on the establishment of new farming acreages in the savannah zones of Ghana. More specifically, the State Farms Corporation should concern itself with the introduction of new crops and proven techniques and establish itself in uncultivated, rather than already farmed areas. This would be an effective means of popularizing new methods and ensuring that idle land resources are put to productive use. In addition, state farms will play a leading part in the production of sugar cane, cotton, rubber, non-apparel fibers and meat where large-scale organization has decided advantages in production."

University of Wisconsin-trained economist Ann Seidman working alongside Reginald H. Green at the University of Ghana-Legon from 1962-66 sought to provide an academic framework for the Nkrumaist vision of African Unification and Socialism. Understanding the significance of rejecting the western orthodoxy of economic theory and its applicability to Africa, Seidman and Green worked to provide the empirical data to verify that integration of continental states was a prerequisite to genuine growth and development.

Of course this viewpoint fell into institutional disfavor after the CIA and State Department engineered coup of February 1966. Moreover, the failure to recognize imperialism as the central impediment to African unification and progress hampers any assessment of why the First Republic efforts were thwarted. After 1966, even Seidman and Green in their published 1968 book "Unity or Poverty?: The Economics of Pan-Africanism", attempts to dislodge the imperatives of African integration from its political and ideological basis. The systematic underdevelopment of Africa is a direct result of the centuries-long legacy of slavery, colonialism and neo-colonialism. In order for Africa to advance economically the basis of its continuing exploitation and oppression must be overthrown.

These are clearly political questions that lead to economic visions and solutions and not vice-versa. Without a strategic outlook informed by an anti-imperialist ideological orientation the concept of African unity and economic integration can never come into view.

Furthermore by ignoring or even denying the role of the principal architect of neo-colonialism and imperialism in the second half of the 20th century extending to the first two decades of the 21th century, leaves the African workers, youth and farmers without the ideological underpinning to challenge the status quo. The inability of African states to develop sustainable economic growth and transformation cannot be explained solely from the perspectives of technological, managerial and skill deficiencies. All former and currently existing Socialist states have been plagued by the same challenges and have overcome them as in China, Democratic Korea, Cuba, Vietnam and other areas where advancements have been made even without the realization of a Socialist society, as in African states breaking the chains of European domination.

Seidman in co-authoring a paper on "State Farms in Ghana" with Marvin P. Miracle concludes correctly in the first instance saying: "In sum, Ghana's state farms programs strongly suggests that for any large-scale farming projects to succeed in Africa there must be careful prior research, adequate numbers of managerial personnel, and trained technicians, and availability of all the complementary resources and marketing facilities." Nevertheless, these two scholars unfortunately fall into a "technocratic" mode of analysis that nullifies the conceptual basis for Pan-Africanism and Socialism in Africa by stressing that "Initially, at least, such projects should probably be limited to those tree crops and industrial raw materials associated with given processing facilities. Where possible, efforts should be made to stimulate private production of additional supplies." (p. 46)

From an ideological standpoint this form of economic logic leads right into providing a rationale for what became known as "Neo-Liberal" reforms which took hold when the so-called National Liberation Council" was installed by the CIA and State Department after the police and military coup. Seidman and Green emphasize that: "In the last analysis, all the financial resources of the state (and of Ghana were, for Africa, extensive) are not adequate to meet all the expanding food and raw material needs of a developing economy by means of state-owned projects. If the Government of Ghana had used the same amount of money and organizational talent that were expended on the state farm program to develop techniques and provide incentives for small farmers, there would probably have been a far greater increase in domestic food production."

As recent as 2014, in a paper published by Gerardo Serra on the work of Seidman and Green in Ghana before and after the CIA and State Department backed coup, entitled "Continental Visions: Ann Seidman, Reginald H. Green and the Economics of African Unity in 1960s Ghana", the author makes what can only be interpreted as a political attack on Nkrumaist Pan-Africanism by claiming: "The Kwame Nkrumah Conference Center (of Job 600, as it came to be called since it was the six hundredth project realized by the Ghana National Construction Corporation) estimated to cost between 8 million and 10 million British pounds at a time where foreign exchange reserves were exhausted and shortages of basic goods were plaguing the economy 'became the symbol of all Nkrumah's foolish prestige projects'. Amidst this atmosphere of increasing popular discontent at home and isolation from other African leaders, Nkrumah was overthrown in February 1966. Although the reasons behind the his overthrow had more to do with the mismanagement of the Ghanaian economy than with the tension pervading the Pan-African scene, the revolutionary dream of a Union Government and a continental plan ended with the fall of Nkrumah, while the crowds in Accra were cheering and smashing statues of the former leader."

In following this clearly pessimistic outlook on the capacity of Africans to determine their own destiny and failing to mention the well-documented plotting, machinations and execution of a police and military coup by the CIA and State Department, not only distorts the political history of Africa but also conveniently dismisses the ongoing role of imperialism, led by Washington and Wall Street, in blocking and reversing any gains made during the course of the African Revolution since the beginning of the post-World War II period.

The army and police officials who took charge of the government formed an alliance with the opposition forces many of whom campaigned against national independence in 1957 saying Ghana was not prepared for liberation under a unitary political system. Those Ghanaian nationals and expatriates that worked within the context of the CPP-led revolutionary government were rendered unemployed forcing many into poverty and exile.

Graham Du Bois was placed under house arrest and soon left the country for Egypt. First Lady Madam Fathia Nkrumah was transported back to her Egyptian home in a plane sent by the government of President Gamal Abdel Nasser.

African Americans such as Julian Mayfield and other progressives from the U.S. were forced to abandon projects established by the Nkrumah government. The ideological orientation of the so-called "National Liberation Council" was clearly pro-imperialist since they owed their existence to the extra-legal actions of the CIA and U.S. State Department.

John Stockwell, a former CIA operative, said of the American involvement in the coup in 1966 that: "Howard Bane, who was the CIA station chief in Accra, engineered the overthrow of Kwame Nkrumah. Inside the CIA it was quite clear. Howard Bane got a double promotion, and was awarded the Intelligence Star for the overthrow of Kwame. The magic of it was that Howard Bane had enough imagination and drive to run this operation without ever documenting what he was doing and there wasn't one shred of paper that was generated that would name the CIA hierarchy as being responsible."(Quote printed in Ghanaweb.com from author of In Search of Enemies, 1978)

The overall status of women in post-coup Ghana was catastrophic with the dismissal of parliament and the removal of cabinet ministers. Most of the women involved in the CPP remained barred and alienated from Ghana politics.

Consequently, the domestic and international influence of women declined. Whereas under the Nkrumah government as early as 1959, African American artist and writer Elton C. Fax wrote in the New York Age of his meeting with Federation of Women Secretary General Dr. Evelyn Armarteifio in Ghana who asked him why Blacks in the U.S. continued to refer to themselves as "Negroes" when the term Afro-American was more appropriate. This sentiment was reflected in the CPP press where the term "Negro" was generally not used.

Such an encounter by Fax while he sketched this woman leader who said to him that she had lived and studied in the U.S., was deemed significant enough by veteran Barbadian-born Socialist and Nationalist leader Richard B. Moore of Harlem to utilize the quote from the New York Age article in his book entitled "The Name Negro: It's Origins and Evil Use", published in 1960. (p. 92)

Six years later in 1965, the Assistant Director of the National Council of Ghana Women, Agatha Dumolga, visited the U.S. as a representative of the Nkrumah government. She was one of 15 women selected to visit over a period of 11 weeks.

Making an impression on the Memphis Commercial Appeal newspaper journalist Elinor Kelley when Dumolga visited this Southern city in July 1965, an article featuring her begins by stating: "Women are taking on more responsibility in running at least one country and they're getting plenty of help from their parliament. Social welfare is the big area where women are making their presence felt in the government of Ghana on the West African coast." (July 15, p. 15)

Kelley reported that Dumolga was visiting supermarkets "to see how food was displayed. She will be in Memphis one week visiting welfare agencies, Juvenile Court, hospitals and talking to women's groups in an idea exchange program. Miss Dumolga said 30 of the 114 members of Ghana's parliament are women. 'The women speak for the women and the men speak for the men', she said."

The writer noted Dumolga was adorned in traditional attire from Ghana as her picture appears in the Commercial Appeal wearing a dress made of kente cloth, carrying a fashionable purse and wearing her hair in a similar style as many African American women would in 1965. Dumolga was quoted as saying: "We have all these things— homes for children, juvenile courts, hospitals, in my own country. But I want to compare the way things are done here and at home."

This same article surmises that: "In Ghana, Miss Dumolga does work that might be compared with a home demonstration agent in the United States. She goes from town to town, teaching women about balanced diets, gardening and sewing. Women are best suited for this. It's easier to make contacts with the women because they take care of the whole house. If they have the understanding they can pass it on to the family."

The report ends noting that Dumolga was the guest of Mrs. Emalyn Myles of 1390 Chadwick Circle, who was a member of the African American women's sorority Delta Sigma Theta, which was co-sponsoring the tour with the African Women's Corps.

Although some of the myths fostered by the NLC and its imperialist backers were that Ghana faced bankruptcy, the deployment of troops to fight in Rhodesia and egregious theft of public resources by Nkrumah himself, these allegations were never proven. The economic conditions inside the country deteriorated in the post-coup period and the clout that Ghana held within Africa and the entire African world has never been retrieved after five decades of both military and civilian rule.

After February 24, 1966, Nkrumah settled in Guinea-Conakry where he was appointed Co-President by the Secretary General Ahmed Sekou Toure of the Democratic Party of Guinea (PDG), a fraternal organization. Nkrumah wrote several pioneering theoretical works during the 1966-1971 period while in Guinea. His writings remain an inspiration to revolutionaries throughout the continent and the international community.

President Toure hosted Nkrumah until 1971 when he was flown to Romania for medical treatment after which he was diagnosed with cancer. Nkrumah died on April 27, 1972 and was given a state funeral by the Guinea government.

Based on certain negotiated conditions, President Toure agreed to send the remains of Nkrumah back to Ghana after being requested for burial by a newly-installed military regime which took power in January 1972. Nkrumah was entombed in his village home of Nkroful in the Nzima region. During the early 1990s, his remains were taken to Accra for burial.

Economic conditions in Ghana had so declined by the mid-1980s that it became the first country to impose the dreaded Structural Adjustment Plans (SAPs) in Africa. The SAPs enacted draconian cuts in education and social services, resulting in the decline of currency values and the further privatization of public assets.

Today the African Union (AU) has passed resolutions mandating the participation of women in the political, economic and educational affairs of member-states. Although progress has been made in several states, there is much to be desired. Africa remains under the domination of international finance capital and any movement towards genuine unification and continental socialist development can only occur after a fundamental break with world capitalism.

The Nkrumah years of transition from 1951-1956 and the independence period of 1957-1966, set the standard for African development and political imperatives related to inter-state integration and Women's affairs. In 1999, former Libyan leader Col. Muammar Gaddafi hosted an OAU Summit in Sirte, which drafted resolutions that would bring about the transition from the old continental group to the AU. Many of the aims and objectives of Nkrumah's Ghana were adopted, if only on a symbolic level, at Sirte in 1999. Subsequently, the first U.S. president of African descent, Barack Obama, serving the interests of the ruling class and the Pentagon, led in the military and economic destruction of this state which was bombed for seven months in 2011 with the approval of the UN Security Council.

Libya, like Ghana before it, illustrates the dangerous nature of imperialism in Africa. Nkrumah in last book published while he was in office entitled "Neo-Colonialism: The Last Stage of Imperialism", correctly identifies the U.S. as the principal enemy of Pan-Africanism and Socialism.

In 2016, with the decline in commodity prices and the increasing military and intelligence penetration of Africa, a struggle must be waged to guarantee the sovereignty and economic independence of the continent. This will prove to be the major challenge of the initial decades of the 21$^{st}$ century not only for Africa but for all oppressed nations and peoples of the world.

www.ingramcontent.com/pod-product-compliance
Lightning Source LLC
Chambersburg PA
CBHW070231290526

45789CB00004B/1570